WORSHIP ONE ON ONE

- 21 Day Devotional -

PROPHETESS HELEN MARIE JONES

Copyright © 2025 by Prophetess Helen Marie Jones

All rights reserved.

No part of this book may be used or reproduced by any means, graphic, electronic, or mechanical, including photocopying, recording, taping, or by any information storage retrieval system, without the written permission of the publisher except in the case of brief quotations embodied in critical articles and reviews.

TABLE OF CONTENTS

Day 1: I am Worship 5

Day 2: Emotions and Worship VS. Feeling and Expression 9

Day 3: Is Your Worship Finding You? 17

Day 4: Turn Up the Volume in Your Worship! 23

Day 5: Declarations & Decrees 31

Day 6: Reach For IT 36

Day 7: My Life Is in Position 39

Day 8: Declare Who You Are in Jesus Christ 42

Day 9: God's Grace in a Genesis Season 47

Day 10: Where Are You Seated? 51

Day 11: Dig Deeper in Worship 54

Day 12: Worship Can Find You In a Safe Place 56

Day 13: A Place Called Worship 59

Day 14: Worship Brings Forth Healing 65

Day 15: Worship That Causes You to Rest 70

Day 16: The Heart of True Worship 75

Day 17: Learning Other Types of Worship 79

Day 18: Personal vs. Corporate Worship 84

Day 19: Corporate Worship 92

Day 20: A Worship Leader Carries a Unique Sound 96

Day 21: I Am Who God Says I Am 100

Meet the Author 102

DAY 1

I am Worship

When Worship Becomes Your Lifestyle

Have you ever been asked a question about who you are and you did not know how to respond at that moment? That is what happens to a lot of us in today's world. Do we know who we are? When we say I am worship, we acknowledge that prayer is fixed in our identity and lifestyle. It is not just something we do but who we are. Our whole being – our actions, thoughts, and interactions is dedicated to glorifying God.

By embracing this truth, we live in constant worship, reflecting His glory in everything we do. I am reminded of when I was in a very dark place. I had a tough childhood; I had no father around me, and my mother and I did not have the best relationship because of what she went through with my father. I remember growing up feeling alone, abandoned, lost, and like no one loved me. Feeling like an orphan child, as a child, I felt so alone. I remember hearing my grandmother pray.

> **Deuteronomy 31:6**: Be strong and courageous. Do not be afraid or terrified because of them, for the LORD your God goes with you; He will never leave you nor forsake you.

Worship is when the Word of God becomes real in your spirit. It is so real that it becomes more than three songs and hype; it becomes who you are, which is a lifestyle. It will become who you are that you can live, breathe, and accept that you are WORSHIP!

When I say I am worship, I emphasize that worship is not merely an action we perform or an event we attend but an integral part of our identity and daily life. Here's a deeper exploration of this concept:

I Am Worship– A Deeper Meaning

Worship is not confined to singing songs or attending church services. It involves offering our entire lives to God as a living sacrifice. Our actions, thoughts, decisions, and lifestyles should reflect our devotion to Him.

Living Sacrifice:

Scripture: Romans 12:1 (NIV) - Therefore, I urge you, brothers and sisters, in view of God's mercy, to offer your bodies as a living sacrifice, holy and pleasing to God–this is your true and proper worship.

Identity in Christ:

Scripture: 1 Peter 2:9 (NIV) - But you are a chosen people, a royal priesthood, a holy nation, God's special possession, that you may declare the praises of him who called you out of darkness into his wonderful light."

Our identity in Christ is foundational to our worship. As God's chosen people, our very existence is meant to declare His praises. Everything we do should stem from our identity as His children and reflect His glory.

Continuous Devotion:

Scripture: 1 Thessalonians 5:16-18 (NIV) - Rejoice always, pray continually, give thanks in all circumstances; for this is God's will for you in Christ Jesus.

Worship is continuous. It's an ongoing expression of our relationship with God. Whether through prayer, thanksgiving, or rejoicing our daily activities become acts of worship when done with a heart oriented toward God.

Heart and Spirit:

Scripture: John 4:23-24 (NIV) - Yet a time is coming and has now come when the true worshipers will worship the Father in the Spirit and truth, for they are the kind of worshipers the Father seeks. God is spirit, and his worshipers must worship in the Spirit and in truth."

True worship comes from the heart and is guided by the Holy Spirit. It's not just about external actions but about an internal posture of reverence, love, and obedience towards God.

I Am Worship

1. **Daily Actions:** Every action, no matter how small, can be an act of worship if done with the right heart. Whether you're working, studying, or helping others, do it as if you're serving God.

2. **Relationships:** Treat others with love, kindness, and respect, reflecting God's love. Building and maintaining godly relationships is a form of worship.

3. **Mindset:** Cultivate a mindset of gratitude and praise. Instead of focusing on problems, focus on God's goodness and faithfulness.

4. **Obedience:** Follow God's commandments and teachings daily. Obedience to His word is a profound expression of worship.

Worship is a Lifestyle

Worship is a part of your life that you must always be ready for.

Make worship a habit. Your worship and revelation come from spending time with God. Describe your place of Worship!

Notes

_____

_____

_____

_____

_____

_____

_____

DAY 2

Emotions and Worship
vs.
Feeling and Expression

When I discovered the concept of worship, I realized the true essence of a genuine and honest relationship. Worship, when defined, is both a feeling and an expression. It serves as a conduit for personal emotions, often manifesting in a range of states like joy, tears, exultation, humility, or shame.

Navigating my relationship with worship posed a challenge – understanding how to feel and express myself authentically. While feeling involves touching and expressing, my life story turned from this type. My emotions remained concealed beneath the weight of unspoken pain as I struggled to communicate my experiences.

My early encounters with touch were distorted, marred by inappropriate experiences as a child. Consequently, my perception of genuine touch was distorted. Sharing and expressing my feelings became a difficult task, hindered by the treatment I endured. The lingering question persisted:

How could I find true feeling and expression in worship?

Recalling the story of the woman with the blood issue, I was inspired by her courage to step out despite uncertainties. Like her, my longing for healing compelled me to reach out and touch the symbolic hem of Jesus' garment.

The foundational step is to have faith and "Step Out," even without clarity about the outcome. Emotions, as David demonstrated, can be a healthy means of connecting with and experiencing God on an emotional level.

Notes

_____
_____
_____
_____
_____
_____
_____
_____
_____
_____

REFLECTION

1. Whom or what do you typically rely on to fulfill your emotional needs, apart from your relationship with God?

_____
_____
_____
_____
_____
_____

2. Why do you find yourself turning to those sources instead of turning to God?

_____
_____
_____
_____
_____
_____
_____

David, known as a man after God's own heart, often turned to worship during times of emotional turmoil. His life was marked by highs and lows, but in those moments, he consistently directed his emotions toward God through worship. Here's how David turned to worship during his emotional struggles:

1. Acknowledging His Emotions

Scripture: How long, Lord? Will you forget me forever? How long will you hide your face from me? How long must I wrestle with my thoughts and have sorrow in my heart daily?

This was a hard place for me, but I found myself like David. David was honest with God about his feelings. He did not hide his sorrow, fear, or frustration. Instead, he brought them before the Lord, acknowledging his emotional state. This openness laid the foundation for his worship as he sought God's presence in his pain.

2. Turning to God in Prayer

Scripture: Psalm 18:6 (NIV)

In my distress, I called to the Lord; I cried to my God for help. From his temple he heard my voice; my cry came before him, into his ears.

In times of distress, David turned to God in prayer. He cried out for help, believing that God heard him. Prayer was a crucial part of David's worship, allowing him to connect with God and find solace.

3. Expressing Trust in God
Scripture: Psalm 56:3-4 (NIV)

When I am afraid, I put my trust in you. In God, whose word I praise—in God I trust and am not afraid. What can mere mortals do to me?

Despite his fears, David chose to trust in God. Worship for David often involved reaffirming his faith and trust in God's promises. By declaring his trust, David shifted his focus from his problems to God's faithfulness.

4. Praising God Amidst the Pain
Scripture: Psalm 34:1 (NIV)

I will always extol the Lord; his praise will always be on my lips.

David deliberately chose to praise God even in difficult times. His worship depended not on his circumstances but on God's unchanging nature. By praising God, David found strength and encouragement.

5. Remembering God's Past Faithfulness
Scripture: Psalm 77:11-12 (NIV)

I will remember the deeds of the Lord; yes, I will remember your miracles of long ago. I will consider all your works and meditate on all your mighty deeds.

David often reflected on God's past deeds and miracles. This remembrance fueled his worship, reminding him of God's power and faithfulness. It gave him hope and assurance that God would deliver him again.

6. Seeking God's Presence
Scripture: Psalm 63:1 (NIV)

You, God, are my God, earnestly I seek you; I thirst for you, my whole being longs for you, in a dry and parched land where there is no water.

David's longing for God's presence was a central aspect of his worship. In times of emotional dryness, he earnestly sought God, knowing that true satisfaction and peace could only be found in Him.

7. Singing and Playing Music
Scripture: Psalm 57:7-9 (NIV)

My heart, O God, is steadfast, my heart is steadfast; I will sing and make music. Awake, my soul! Awake, harp and lyre! I will awaken the dawn. I will praise you, Lord, among the nations; I will sing of you among the peoples.

David often expressed his worship through singing and playing instruments. Music was a powerful outlet for his emotions and a means to glorify God. It helped him to refocus his mind and heart on God's goodness. David's approach to worship during emotional struggles serves as a powerful example for us. By acknowledging his emotions, turning to God in prayer, expressing trust, praising God amidst the pain, remembering God's faithfulness, seeking His presence, and using music, David found relief and strength in worship. His life demonstrates that worship is a profound way to navigate and transcend our emotional challenges, drawing us closer to God and His enduring love. My spiritual father, the late Bishop Gregory Carter, used to speak a profound word to me: Jones, you must SING YOUR WAY OUT. At the time, I didn't realize that my gift for singing would be the key to overcoming my distress and leading me into worship. Now, I understand that when you acknowledge who you are and recognize your pain, that pain can guide you to your purpose and calling.

What is the deep pain that's holding you back from worship?

_____
_____
_____
_____
_____
_____
_____

How can you use worship as a tool to shift your focus from your pain to God's presence?

_____
_____
_____
_____
_____
_____
_____

David found strength in worship during difficult times. How can you incorporate music or praise into your daily life to help you stay steadfast in your faith?

_____
_____
_____
_____
_____
_____
_____

Reflecting on Bishop Gregory Carter's words, "Sing your way out," how can you use your gifts—whether singing, writing, or another form of worship—to overcome challenges and walk in your purpose?

_____
_____
_____
_____
_____
_____
_____

DAY 3

Is Your Worship Finding You?

But the hour cometh, and now is, when the true worshippers shall worship the Father in spirit and in truth: for the Father seeketh such to worship him. John 4: 23 -24

When I was a little girl, we used to play a game called Hiding Go Seek. The object of the game was to find someone that is hiding. When God comes looking for you in worship, will he find you hiding OR WORSHIPPING? There was a time when I had to examine myself. After researching my life, I realized that I was hiding from worship. Early one Monday morning, the Lord awakened me. I kept hearing in my ear early in the morning will I seek thee. At that moment, I felt I needed to enter a place of holy holy. I realized God needed me to set aside my Do List and be still before his presence. I laid aside my agenda and soaked in his presence at that moment. At that moment, Worship found me.

God is a Spirit, and they who worship him must worship him in spirit and in truth.

In reality, I discovered that worship is more than just music. God is seeking someone who is unadulterated, pure, and true. When we get to that place in God, we bring God Glory. Worship must come from your spirit within instead of being merely formal and external. John 3:6 reminds us that Jesus connects God's Spirit and our spirit in a remarkable way. He says that which is born of the Spirit is spirit. Only that which is born of the Spirit is spirit. So, when Jesus says that true worshipers worship in spirit, he must mean that true worship only comes from spirits that are made alive and sensitive and vital by the touch of the Holy Spirit.

True worship is about the heart and spirit being aligned with God, rather than the external aspects. It's easy to get distracted by the rituals, styles, or appearances, but worship is ultimately about connecting with God in a genuine, humble way. Jesus even said that true worshipers will worship the Father in "spirit and in truth" (John 4:24), which emphasizes sincerity and authenticity in our relationship with God over outward formalities. In moments of deep sadness, you may start singing a hymn or a worship song that speaks of God's faithfulness. As you sing, your focus shifts from your pain to God's promises, and you begin to experience His comforting presence.

1. During Times of Joy
Worship can find you in moments of great joy and celebration. When your heart is full of gratitude, worship naturally flows from a place of thankfulness. It's a spontaneous response to the goodness and blessings you recognize in your life.

When you receive good news or witness a miracle, you might lift your hands in praise, thanking God for His blessings. This act of worship deepens your joy and acknowledges God as the source of your happiness.

2. In the Routine of Daily Life

Worship can find you in the routine activities of everyday life. As you go about your daily tasks, an awareness of God's presence can transform ordinary moments into acts of worship. It's about cultivating a heart of gratitude and mindfulness in everything you do. While doing chores, driving to work, or taking a walk, you might find yourself thanking God for the simple things in life. This continuous attitude of gratitude turns your everyday actions into worship.

3. Through Nature and Creation

Worship can find you as you marvel at the beauty of creation. The awe-inspiring sights and sounds of nature can lead you to a place of reverence and worship, as you recognize the Creator behind the creation. Standing on a mountaintop, watching a sunset, or listening to the waves crash against the shore can prompt you to worship God for His magnificent handiwork. You feel connected to Him and His creation in a profound way.

4. In Community with Others

Worship can find you in the company of fellow believers. Gathering with others to sing, pray, and share God's Word can ignite a collective spirit of worship. The unity and encouragement found in the community can draw you into a deeper experience of worship.

During a church service or small group meeting, the collective voices lifted in praise can create a powerful atmosphere of worship. The shared experience strengthens your faith and draws you closer to God.

6. In Moments of Reflection

Worship can find you in quiet moments of reflection and meditation. Taking time to sit in silence, read Scripture, or journal your thoughts can open your heart to God's presence, leading to a personal and intimate form of worship. In the early morning or late at night, you might find a quiet spot to reflect on God's goodness and faithfulness. As you meditate on His Word and pray, your heart naturally turns to worship. Worship can find you in sorrow, joy, routine, nature, community, and reflection. It's not confined to a specific place or time but can occur anywhere and anytime. By being open to God's presence and recognizing His hand in all aspects of life, you allow worship to find you and transform your heart, drawing you closer to Him.

Notes

_____

_____

_____

_____

_____

_____

REFLECTION

1. In what ways has worship found you in unexpected moments of joy or gratitude, and how did it deepen your connection with God?

_____
_____
_____
_____
_____
_____
_____

2. How can you cultivate a heart of worship in your daily routine, turning ordinary moments into opportunities to glorify God?

_____
_____
_____
_____
_____
_____
_____

3. Reflecting on how nature reveals God's handiwork, what aspects of creation have inspired you to worship, and how can you be more intentional in seeing God's presence around you?

_____
_____
_____
_____
_____
_____
_____

4. Where can God find you in worship?

_____
_____
_____
_____
_____
_____
_____
_____

DAY 4

Turn Up the Volume in Your Worship!

How loud is your sound? Is your volume up or down? You can worship quietly and still praise loudly, it is all about how your life looks, what it reflects, and whether it is lived in inspired praise because that is what it means to praise loudly. Matthew 5:14–16 tells us, "You are the light of the world. A town built on a hill cannot be hidden. Neither do people light a lamp and put it under a bowl. Instead, they put it on its stand, and it gives light to everyone in the house. In the same way, let your light shine before others, that they may see your good deeds and glorify your Father in heaven." In other words, Jesus was saying that once we have crossed over from darkness into light, from death into life, we need to take that new life and live it loud, having the courage to be who God is making us to be and not worrying what other people think about it.

> Sing to the LORD a new song, for he has done marvelous things; his right hand and his holy arm have worked salvation for him. **Psalm 98:1–9 NIV**

The LORD has made his salvation known and revealed his righteousness to the nations. He has remembered his love and his faithfulness to Israel; all the ends of the earth have seen the salvation of our God. Shout for joy to the LORD, all the earth, burst into jubilant song with music; make music to the LORD with the harp, with the harp and the sound of singing, with trumpets and the blast of the ram's horn– shout for joy before the LORD, the King. Let the sea resound, and everything in it, the world, and all who live in it. Let the rivers clap their hands, let the mountains sing together for joy; let them sing before the LORD, for he comes to judge the earth. He will judge the world in righteousness and the peoples with equity. To turn up the volume in worship, both figuratively and literally, means to deepen and intensify your worship experience. Here are some ways to do that:

A. Engage Your Heart Fully- Worship begins with the heart. Engage fully by being present and intentional in your worship. Reflect on God's attributes, His goodness, and His works in your life.

How:

- Spend time in prayer before worship to prepare your heart.
- Reflect on specific reasons you are grateful to God.
- Meditate on His Word to remind yourself of His promises and character.

B. Express Yourself Freely- Be bold in expressing your worship. Whether you sing, raise your hands, or even dance, let your body reflect the intensity of your worship.

How:

- Sing loudly and passionately.
- Use physical expressions like raising your hands, kneeling, or clapping.
- If you're comfortable, dance or move in a way that reflects your joy and reverence.

C. Deepen Your Understanding of God- Worship is enriched by knowing who God is. The more you understand His nature and His works, the deeper your worship can become.

How:

- Study the Bible regularly to learn more about God's character and His deeds.
- Read books or listen to sermons that explore theological concepts and God's nature.
- Reflect on God's attributes like His love, justice, mercy, and power.

D. Cultivate a Lifestyle of Worship- Worship is not confined to a service or a song; it's a way of life. Live in a way that honors God and reflects His love and grace.

How:

- Make worship a daily practice, not just a Sunday activity.
- Serve others and live out your faith in practical ways.
- Let your decisions and actions be guided by your devotion to God.

E. Seek God's Presence- Desire and seek God's presence earnestly. Worship is about connecting with Him, and this connection deepens as you draw nearer to Him.

How:

- Spend time in personal prayer and devotion.
- Create a quiet space where you can be alone with God.
- Be still and listen for His voice during your worship.

F. Worship in Spirit and Truth- True worshipers worship in spirit and truth. This means worshiping sincerely and based on the truth of who God is, as revealed in Scripture.

How:

- Align your worship with Biblical truths.
- Let your worship be genuine, not just an outward display.
- Focus on the Holy Spirit's guidance and promptings during worship.

G Join with Others in Worship- There is power in corporate worship. Joining with others can amplify the worship experience as you encourage and uplift one another.

How:

- Participate actively in church services and group worship sessions.
- Share testimonies and experiences of God's work in your life.
- Encourage and pray for one another, fostering a community of worship.

H. Use Your Gifts and Talents- God has given each person unique gifts and talents. Use these in your worship to glorify Him and enhance the worship experience for yourself and others.

How:

- If you have musical talents, use them to lead or participate in worship.
- Use creative arts like painting, writing, or dance as expressions of worship.
- Serve in your church or community in ways that reflect your skills and passions.

<u>**David reminds us:**</u>

- Remember the good things that God has done for you.
- Think about God's provision of salvation.
- Remember God's faithfulness.
- Think about the joy that is ours in Christ.
- Look at the creation around us.
- In distress, call upon the Lord.

Turning up the volume in worship involves engaging your heart, expressing yourself freely, deepening your understanding of God, cultivating a lifestyle of worship, seeking His presence, worshiping in spirit and truth, joining with others, and using your gifts. By doing these things, you can experience a more profound and impactful worship that honors God and enriches your relationship with Him. Worship is more than a song—it's a posture, a surrender, and a declaration of who God is in our lives. When we worship, we shift the atmosphere, break strongholds, and invite the presence of God to dwell among us. True worship isn't about perfection; it's about devotion. It's about lifting our voices, even in brokenness, and offering God the praise He deserves.

This song by Phil Thompson reminds us that worship is not optional—it's essential. *"And I will not be silent, I will always worship You."* These lyrics ignite something deep within me, pushing me to worship God with my whole heart, regardless of what I'm facing. This song has been a personal anthem, a reminder that as long as I have breath in my body, my worship will not be silenced. I encourage you today—turn up your volume of worship. Lift your hands, open your mouth, and let your praise rise! Here's a song to help you do just that. Let it minister to you, let it transform you, and let your worship become the sound that shifts your life.

Song Writer Phil Thompson

And I will not be silent

I will always worship You

As long as I am breathing

I will always worship You

REFLECTION

1. What songs help you turn up the volume on your worship?

_____
_____
_____
_____
_____
_____

2. What does "turning up the volume in worship" look like for you, and how can you engage more fully in expressing your devotion to God?

_____
_____
_____
_____
_____
_____
_____

3. Think about a time when worship helped you shift the atmosphere in your life. How did it impact your emotions, circumstances, or relationship with God?

_____

_____

_____

_____

_____

_____

4. Phil Thompson's song declares, "I will not be silent." What are some things in your life that have tried to silence your worship, and how can you push past them to give God the praise He deserves?

_____

_____

_____

_____

_____

_____

DAY 5

Declarations & Decrees

Scriptures for Study

- **Revelation 2-3**

- **Ephesians 3:10**

- **Esther 8:10-13**

Prayer

In the Name of Jesus Christ, with His authority and by His power, I release these decrees. The angelic hosts are ready to carry them out in the heavenly realms—before rulers and authorities—and to proclaim them in the King's palace. Empowered by the Holy Spirit, we dispatch the angelic hosts throughout this land and the spiritual realms to deliver these decrees to all, both flesh and spirit. The enemy, principalities, and powers have no authority to resist the decrees of the King, the Lord God Almighty. Their actions will have no effect on God's chosen ones but will be turned back on themselves for destruction. Lord God Almighty, Maker of Heaven and Earth, we praise Your Holy Name, for You are faithful and true to bring these decrees to pass. In Jesus' name Amen!

Notes

_____
_____
_____
_____
_____
_____
_____
_____
_____
_____
_____
_____
_____
_____

DECLARATIONS

1. **I decree and declare** that you, servants of the Most High God, have a deep desire to obey His laws, rulings, and commandments with all your heart and being. The Lord is your God, and you walk in His ways, doing as He commands.

2. **I decree and declare** that you are the Lord's own treasured possession. As you follow Him, He will lift you high above all nations He has created, in praise, reputation, and glory. You will be a holy people, set apart for the Lord your God.

3. **I declare** that the Lord is my God! I exalt and praise Your name, Lord, for You have done marvelous things, fulfilling ancient plans faithfully and truthfully.

4. **I decree and declare** that mighty nations will glorify the Lord Most High; ruthless nations will fear Him. He is a refuge for the poor and needy, a shelter from the storm, and a shade from the heat.

5. **I decree and declare** that true worshipers will worship the Father in spirit and in truth, for these are the kind of people the Father seeks to worship Him. God is Spirit, and His worshipers must worship Him in spirit and truth.

6. **I declare** that the Lord, my God, is worthy of all praise, glory, and honor! I worship Him in the beauty of His holiness.

7. **I declare** that the voice of the Lord is upon the waters; the God of glory thunders! The voice of the Lord is powerful and majestic over the rushing waters.

8. **I decree and declare** that the voice of the Lord strikes with fiery flames; it shakes the wilderness and makes the desert tremble. All in His temple cry, "Glory!" The Lord reigns above the flood; He is enthroned as King forever!

9. **I declare** that from God's throne come flashes of lightning, voices, and thundering! The four living creatures never cease to say, "Holy, holy, holy is the Lord God Almighty, who was, and is, and is to come!"

10. **I declare** that as the living creatures give glory, honor, and thanks to the One seated on the throne, who lives forever and ever, the twenty-four elders fall down and worship Him, casting their crowns before the throne, saying, "You are worthy, our Lord and God, to receive glory, honor, and power, for You created all things, and by Your will they exist and were created!"

11. **I declare** a cleansing and unification of the people of this land as these decrees go forth.

Write yours below:

DAY 6

Reach For IT

David was a man after God's heart in studying the scripture no matter what he was facing, and he began to Reach for the Father in songs and prayer because he knew it was God who was going to bring him out. Reach for what's on the inside and pull out what God is saying. David had a cry that reached the heavens. In Psalms 40: 1-4 David proclaimed:

I waited patiently for the LORD to help me, and he turned to me and heard my cry. He lifted me out of the pit of despair, out of the mud and the mire. He set my feet on solid ground and steadied me as I walked along. He has given me a new song to sing, a hymn of praise to our God. Many will see what he has done and be amazed. They will put their trust in the LORD.

Ways to Reach True Worship

Achieving true worship is often a personal and subjective journey that varies across different religious or spiritual beliefs. Here are some general principles that many people find helpful:

- **Study Sacred Texts**: Understand and study the sacred texts or teachings associated with your faith. This helps in gaining knowledge about the principles and practices of your religion.

- **Prayer and Meditation**: Regular prayer or meditation is a common practice in many religions. It allows individuals to connect with the divine, seek guidance, and cultivate a sense of inner peace.

- **Attend Religious Services**: Participate in religious services, rituals, or gatherings. These communal activities often foster a sense of community and shared spirituality.

- **Live by Honorable Values**: Practicing ethical values and moral conduct is often considered an integral part of true worship. Treat others with kindness, compassion, and respect.

- **Reflect and Self-Examination**: Take time for self-reflection and self-examination. Understand your beliefs, actions, and intentions. This introspection can lead to personal growth and a deeper connection with your faith.

- **Serve Others**: Many religions emphasize the importance of serving others. Engaging in acts of kindness and helping those in need can be a form of worship.

- **Cultivate Gratitude**: Expressing gratitude for the blessings in your life is a way to acknowledge the divine and cultivate a positive mindset.

- **Seek Guidance from Spiritual Leaders**: Consult with spiritual leaders or mentors within your faith community. They can provide guidance, answer questions, and offer support on your spiritual journey.

Remember that the path to true worship is unique for each individual. It's essential to be open-minded, tolerant, and respectful of diverse beliefs and practices. If you have specific religious or spiritual traditions in mind, it may be helpful to consult with leaders or experts within those traditions for more personalized guidance.

Notes

_____
_____
_____
_____
_____
_____
_____
_____
_____
_____
_____
_____
_____

DAY 7

My Life Is in Position

A lifestyle of worship can take many forms depending on an individual's religious or spiritual tradition, but at its core, it involves living in a way that reflects a deep reverence and dedication to one's beliefs and the divine. A lifestyle of worship refers to a way of living where an individual or a community consistently and intentionally expresses their devotion, reverence, and gratitude to a deity, higher power, or spiritual belief system through various practices, attitudes, and behaviors. This lifestyle is characterized by a deep and continuous connection to one's faith or spirituality, and it often involves the following elements:

Spiritual Practices: Regular spiritual practices, such as prayer, meditation, scripture reading, or rituals, help individuals connect with their beliefs and deepen their relationship with the divine.

Gratitude and Thankfulness: Cultivating an attitude of gratitude and thankfulness for the blessings and experiences in life, acknowledging that everything comes from a higher source.

Moral and Ethical Values: Upholding a set of moral and ethical principles that align with one's faith and striving to live in accordance with these values in everyday life.

Acts of Service and Charity: Demonstrating compassion and love for others through acts of service, charity, and kindness as a way to honor one's beliefs and contribute positively to the world.

Community Involvement: Participating in religious or spiritual communities and gatherings to foster a sense of belonging, support, and shared worship experiences.

Mindfulness and Presence: Practicing mindfulness and being present in the moment, allowing for a deeper connection with the divine and an appreciation of the beauty in the world.

Reflection and Self-Examination: Engaging in self-reflection and introspection to understand one's beliefs, doubts, and spiritual journey, and to continuously grow in faith.

Celebrations and Rituals: Observing religious festivals, rituals, and ceremonies that mark significant milestones and moments in one's faith, reinforcing the worshipful lifestyle.

Continuous Learning: Pursuing ongoing education and spiritual growth, whether through studying sacred texts, attending lectures, or seeking guidance from spiritual mentors.

Consistency and Devotion: Maintaining a consistent commitment to one's spiritual beliefs and practices, even during challenging times, as a way of honoring and worshiping the divine.

Notes

_____
_____
_____
_____
_____
_____
_____
_____
_____
_____
_____
_____
_____

DAY 8

Declare Who You Are in Jesus Christ

It is important for a worship leader to speak affirmations for several key reasons:

1. **Encouragement and Building Faith**: Affirmations remind the congregation of God's promises and truth. They help build faith, especially during challenging times, by focusing the hearts of worshipers on God's goodness, love, and power. Words of affirmation can uplift and inspire, making worship a more meaningful and spirit-filled experience.

2. **Creating Unity in Worship**: A worship leader speaking affirmations unifies the congregation by directing everyone's focus toward God. Affirming truths about God's character and promises fosters a shared sense of purpose and draws people together in collective worship.

3. **Shaping Worship Atmosphere**: The words spoken by a worship leader help set the tone and spiritual atmosphere. Affirmations can encourage an atmosphere of expectancy, joy, or reverence, depending on what is being affirmed about God. This helps guide the congregation into deeper, more intentional worship.

4. **Reinforcing Identity in Christ**: Speaking affirmations reminds believers of their identity in Christ. Worshipers are reminded that they are loved, chosen, and accepted by God. This strengthens their relationship with God and reinforces their sense of belonging in His family.

5. **Leading by Example**: Worship leaders are often seen as spiritual leaders during the service. By speaking affirmations, they model a faith-filled mindset, teaching the congregation how to speak truth over their own lives and situations, both in and outside of worship.

Repeat the following affirmations daily:

1. **I am a child of God.**

2. **I am redeemed from the hand of the enemy.**

3. **I am forgiven.**

4. **I am saved by grace through faith.**

5. **I am justified.**

6. **I am sanctified.**

7. **I am a new creature in Christ Jesus.**

8. I am a partaker of God's divine nature.

9. I am redeemed from the curse of the Law.

10. I am delivered from the power of darkness.

11. I am led by the Holy Spirit.

12. I am kept in safety wherever I go.

13. I have the divine favor of God in whatever I do and wherever I go.

14. I am getting all my needs met by Jesus.

15. I am casting all my cares on Jesus.

16. I am strong in the Lord and in the power of His might.

17. I am doing all things through Jesus Christ who strengthens me.

18. I am an heir of God and a joint heir with Jesus Christ.

19. I am an heir to the blessings of Abraham.

20. I am observing and doing the Lord's commandments.

21. I am blessed coming in and blessed going out.

22. I am an heir of eternal life.

23. I am blessed with all spiritual blessings.

24. I am healed by the stripes of Jesus.

25. I am exercising my authority over the enemy.

26. I am above only and not beneath.

27. I am more than a conqueror.

28. I am establishing God's Word here on earth.

29. I am an overcomer by the blood of the Lamb and the word of my testimony.

30. I am daily overcoming the devil.

31. I am not moved by what I see.

32. I am walking by faith and not by sight.

33. I am casting down vain imaginations.

34. I am bringing every thought into captivity in Christ Jesus.

35. I am being transformed by renewing my mind.

36. I am a laborer together with God.

37. I am the righteousness of God through Jesus Christ.

38. I am the light of the world.

39. I am blessing the Lord always and will continue praising Him with my mouth.

40. I am the head and not the tail.

41. I am putting on the mind of Jesus Christ.

42. I am a continuous blessing to my brothers and sisters in Jesus Christ.

43. I am free from all bondages because the bondage-destroying anointing—the Spirit of God—dwells inside of me; therefore, I am bondage-free.

Notes

_____
_____
_____
_____
_____
_____
_____
_____
_____
_____
_____

DAY 9

God's Grace in a Genesis Season

The earth was formless and empty, and darkness covered the deep waters. And the Spirit of God was hovering over the surface of the waters." (Genesis 1:2 NLT)

As a Worship Leader, you have to be able to experience a Genesis experience. A Genesis season is a time of new beginnings, marked by grace.

1. **Discovery**

    Darkness speaks of mystery—you cannot see the path ahead. But God, whose very presence is light, is going with you. And He will light the way. This is your season of discovery and new beginnings.

2. **Room to Receive**

   Emptiness speaks of a space ready to receive new things. If you feel empty or have recently had a chapter close, it is a sign that you have room to receive.

3. **A Vessel for His Glory**

   Formless, or shapeless, reminds us of the potter and the clay (Isaiah 64:8). As you surrender to God's hands, he will bring shape to your life and work.

As you are developing the new you are beginning to hear a new song, a new sound, a new posture; allow God to take out the old and make you NEW.

> Behold, I am doing a new thing; now it springs forth, do you not perceive it? I will make a way in the wilderness and rivers in the desert. **Isaiah 43:19**

Notes

_____
_____
_____
_____
_____
_____
_____
_____
_____

REFLECTION

1. What areas of your life feel dark or uncertain right now, and how can you trust God to bring light and direction to those places?

_____
_____
_____
_____
_____
_____
_____
_____

2. In what ways has God created space in your life for something new? How can you position yourself to receive His grace and fresh opportunities?

_____
_____
_____
_____
_____
_____
_____
_____

3. How is God shaping and molding you in this season? What old things do you need to release so He can make you new?

DAY 10

Where Are You Seated?

The phrase seated at Jesus' feet is often used symbolically in Christian teachings to express a posture of humility, submission, and a desire to learn from Jesus. It originates from biblical narratives, particularly in the New Testament. In the Gospel of Luke (Luke 10:38-42), there is an account of Jesus visiting the home of two sisters, Mary and Martha. Martha is busy with household chores, while Mary sits at Jesus' feet, listening to his teachings. When Martha expresses her frustration that Mary isn't helping with the chores, Jesus responds that Mary has chosen the "better" thing, implying that seeking spiritual understanding and wisdom is of greater importance. Being seated at Jesus' feet symbolizes a position of discipleship, where one is eager to learn, be guided, and receive spiritual insight directly from Jesus. It reflects a posture of humility, acknowledging Jesus as a teacher or mentor and expressing a deep desire to understand and follow his teachings. Anyone can be seated at the feet of Jesus, as the invitation to draw near to Him is open to all. In a spiritual sense, this act represents coming into His presence with humility, openness, and a heart of worship. Here are a few groups of people who may find particular significance in this posture:

1. The Seeker-Those who are seeking spiritual truth, wisdom, or meaning in life. Jesus is seen as the ultimate source of truth and purpose. Sitting at His feet symbolizes seeking guidance and understanding from the one who is "the way, the truth, and the life" (John 14:6).

2. The Disciple-Followers of Jesus who want to grow deeper in their faith. Like Mary of Bethany, disciples sit at Jesus' feet to learn and grow in spiritual wisdom, prioritizing time with Him and His teachings over worldly concerns (Luke 10:39).

3. The Burdened-Those weighed down by life's challenges, grief, anxiety, or sin. Jesus invites the weary and burdened to come to Him for rest (Matthew 11:28). Sitting at His feet is a posture of surrender, laying down burdens and receiving His peace.

4. The Worshiper-Those who come to offer adoration and praise to Jesus.

Why: Sitting at His feet in worship expresses reverence and awe, recognizing His divinity, goodness, and love. It reflects a desire to honor Jesus with wholehearted devotion.

5. The Repentant-People seeking forgiveness for their sins and restoration.

Why: Sitting at Jesus' feet symbolizes humility and repentance, acknowledging one's need for grace and redemption. Jesus offers forgiveness and new life to all who come to Him with repentance.

6. The Suffering-Those enduring pain, illness, or trials. In suffering, sitting at the feet of Jesus can symbolize seeking comfort, healing, and strength from the one who is compassionate and who understands human suffering deeply.

Ultimately, Jesus' invitation is for everyone, regardless of their background or current circumstances. His love and grace are extended to all who come to Him with an open heart, desiring to learn, worship, or find healing.

Notes

_____
_____
_____
_____
_____
_____
_____
_____
_____
_____
_____
_____
_____

DAY 11

Dig Deeper in Worship

How do we dig deeper in worship?

Remember that the journey of deepening worship is personal, and there is no one-size-fits-all approach. Being open-minded, patient, and sincere in your exploration is essential. Digging deeper in worship is a subjective and personal journey that can vary based on individual beliefs and practices. Here are some general suggestions that might help you explore a deeper connection in worship:

1. **Reflect on Your Beliefs**: Take time to reflect on your beliefs and values. Understanding what you believe in can deepen your connection to your faith or spiritual practices.

2. **Study Sacred Texts**: Engage in the study of sacred texts associated with your faith. This can provide a deeper understanding of the teachings and **principles that guide your worship.**

3. **Prayer and Meditation**: Practice prayer and meditation to create a quiet space for reflection and connection with the divine. This can help you cultivate a deeper sense of spirituality.

4. **Participate in Services and Ceremonies**: Engage in religious rituals and ceremonies that are meaningful to you. These practices often carry deep symbolic significance and can enhance your worship experience.

5. **Community Engagement**: Connect with a community of like-minded individuals. Sharing your spiritual journey with others can provide support and new perspectives on worship.

6. **Seek Guidance**: Consult with religious leaders, mentors, or spiritual guides for guidance on deepening your worship. They may offer insights and advice based on their own experiences.

7. **Express Gratitude**: Cultivate an attitude of gratitude. Recognizing and expressing gratitude for the positive aspects of your life can enhance your spiritual connection.

8. **Serve Others**: Engage in acts of service and kindness. Helping others can be a way to express your faith in action and deepen your connection to a higher purpose.

9. **Explore Different Forms of Worship**: Consider exploring different forms of worship within your faith tradition. This may include attending different types of religious services or incorporating diverse spiritual practices.

DAY 12

Worship Can Find You In a Safe Place

The Lord is a refuge for the oppressed, a stronghold in times of trouble. Those who know your name trust in you, for you, Lord, have never forsaken those who seek you. Sing the praises of the Lord, enthroned in Zion; proclaim among the nations what he has done. Psalm 9:9 -11

Once in my life, I experienced oppression and depression time. Not wanting to live, everything was just going upside down. A PLACE CALL WORSHIP FOUND ME at my lowest. Once you enter authentic worship, Worshiping rekindles and revives the spiritual fire within us. It is an experience of the heart that brings us closer to God and magnifies His name. Worship can find you in a safe place because it creates a strong spiritual connection with the divine, offering reassurance and comfort. The act of worship, whether through prayer, meditation, or communal gatherings, provides emotional healing and a sense of belonging. Regular worship also brings routine and structure, contributing to a stable environment. Additionally, the reflective nature of worship helps individuals gain a deeper understanding of themselves and fosters a positive mindset. This combination of spiritual, emotional, and communal support can help individuals feel secure and protected, no matter their external circumstances. By emphasizing these points, you can convey how worship contributes to a sense of safety and well-being. Explaining how worship can find you in a safe place involves highlighting the spiritual and emotional aspects of worship that provide a sense of security and peace. Here's a way to approach it:

Spiritual Connection
Worship creates a connection with the divine, which can provide a deep sense of security. This connection often brings comfort and reassurance, knowing that a higher power is looking over you.

Emotional Healing
Engaging in worship can be a form of emotional release. Singing, praying, or meditating can help individuals process their feelings and find inner peace. This emotional healing can create a mental safe space where worries and fears are alleviated.

Community and Belonging
Worship often takes place in a community setting. Being surrounded by others who share your beliefs and values can foster a sense of belonging and safety. The support and fellowship found in communal worship can be a source of strength and protection.

Routine and Structure

Regular worship can provide structure and routine, which can be comforting and stabilizing. This consistency can create a predictable and secure environment, contributing to a sense of safety.

Personal Reflection

Worship provides time for personal reflection and introspection. This can help individuals better understand themselves and their place in the world, fostering a sense of inner security and clarity.

Positive Mindset

Engaging in worship can encourage a positive mindset. Many forms of worship emphasize gratitude, hope, and love, which can combat negative thoughts and create a safe mental environment.

Transcendence of Circumstances

Worship allows individuals to transcend their immediate circumstances. By focusing on something greater than themselves, they can gain perspective and feel less overwhelmed by their current challenges, contributing to a feeling of safety.

Notes

_____

_____

_____

_____

DAY 13

A Place Called Worship

The apostle Paul described true worship perfectly in Romans 12:1-2: "I urge you therefore, brethren, by the mercies of God to present your bodies a living and holy sacrifice, acceptable to God which is your spiritual service of worship. Do not conform to this world but be transformed by the renewing of your mind so that you may prove what the will of God is, that which is good and acceptable, or well pleasing and perfect. This passage contains all the elements of true worship.

First, there is the motivation to worship the mercies of God. God's mercies are everything He has given us that we don't deserve eternal love, eternal grace, the Holy Spirit, everlasting peace, eternal joy, saving faith, comfort, strength, wisdom, hope, patience, kindness, honor, glory, righteousness, security, eternal life, forgiveness, reconciliation, justification, sanctification, freedom, intercession and much more. The knowledge and understanding of these incredible gifts motivate us to pour forth praise and thanksgiving–in other words, worship! Also in the passage is a description of the manner of our worship: *Present your body as a living and holy sacrifice. Presenting our bodies means giving to God all of ourselves.*

The reference to our bodies here means all our human faculties, all of our humanness—our hearts, minds, hands, thoughts, and attitudes—are to be presented to God. In other words, we are to give up control of these things and turn them over to Him, just as a literal sacrifice was given totally to God on the altar. But how? By the renewing of your mind. We renew our minds daily by cleansing them of the world's wisdom and replacing it with true wisdom that comes from God. We worship Him with our renewed and cleansed minds, not with our emotions. Emotions are beautiful things, but they can be destructive, out-of-control forces unless they are shaped by a mind saturated in Truth. Where the mind goes, the will follows, and so do the emotions.

I Corinthians 2:16 tells us we have "the mind of Christ," not the emotions of Christ. There is only one way to renew our minds, and that is by the Word of God. It is the truth, the knowledge of the Word of God, which is to say, the knowledge of the mercies of God, and we're back where we began. To know the truth, to believe the truth, to hold convictions about the truth, and to love the truth will naturally result in true spiritual worship. It is conviction followed by affection, affection that is a response to truth, not to any external stimuli, including music. Music, as such, has nothing to do with worship. Music can't produce worship, although it certainly can produce emotion. Music is not the origin of worship, but it can be the expression of it. Do not look to music to induce your worship; look to music as simply an expression of that which is induced by a heart that is rapt by the mercies of God, obedient to His commands.

True worship is God-centered worship. People tend to get caught up in where they should worship, what music they should sing in worship, and how their worship looks to other people. Focusing on these things misses the point. Jesus tells us that true worshipers will worship God in spirit and in truth (John 4:24). This means we worship from the heart and the way God has designed. Worship can include praying, reading God's Word with an open heart, singing, participating in communion, and serving others. It is not limited to one act but is done properly when the heart and attitude of the person are in the right place.

It's also important to know that worship is reserved only for God. Only He is worthy and not any of His servants (Revelation 19:10). We are not to worship saints, prophets, statues, angels, any false gods, or Mary, the mother of Jesus. We also should not be worshiping for the expectation of something in return, such as a miraculous healing. Worship is done for God—because He deserves it—and for His pleasure alone. Worship can be public praise to God (Psalm 22:22; 35:18) in a congregational setting, where we can proclaim through prayer and praise our adoration and thankfulness to Him and what He has done for us. True worship is felt inwardly and then is expressed through our actions. "Worshiping" out of obligation is displeasing to God and is entirely in vain. He can see through all the hypocrisy, and He hates it. He demonstrates this in Amos 5:21-24 as He talks about coming judgment.

Another example is the story of Cain and Abel, the first sons of Adam and Eve. They both brought gift offerings to the Lord, but God was only pleased with Abel's. Cain got the gift out of obligation; Abel brought his finest lambs from his flock. He brought out of faith and admiration for God.

True worship is not confined to what we do in church or open praise (although these things are both good, and we are told in the Bible to do them). True worship is the acknowledgment of God and all His power and glory in everything we do. The highest form of praise and worship is obedience to Him and His Word. To do this, we must know God; we cannot be ignorant of Him (Acts 17:23). Worship is to glorify and exalt God–to show our loyalty and admiration to our Father. Then and only then when we will enter in a place called worship.

Notes

REFLECTION

1. How does presenting your body as a living sacrifice impact your daily walk with God?

_____
_____
_____
_____
_____
_____
_____

2. In what areas of your life do you need to surrender more fully to Him?

_____
_____
_____
_____
_____
_____
_____
_____

3. In what ways can you renew your mind daily to align with God's truth rather than conforming to worldly influences?

_____
_____
_____
_____
_____
_____
_____

4. How can you shift your perspective on worship from external expressions (such as music) to a deeper, heart-centered response to God's mercies

_____
_____
_____
_____
_____
_____
_____
_____

DAY 14

Worship Brings Forth Healing

Your question may be about how this works with being a worship leader. Do you ever wonder how can you lead if you are broken? When you enter healing through worship, you invite the Holy Spirit to come. Healing in worship happens through several interconnected processes. Spiritually, worship connects you with the divine, offering peace and a sense of support. Emotionally, worship allows you to express and release your feelings through prayer, singing, and meditation. The communal aspect of worship provides a supportive network, creating a feeling of belonging and shared strength. Reflective practices within worship help you gain personal insights and promote emotional healing. Positive affirmations during worship can shift your mindset towards hope and positivity. The routines and rituals of worship bring stability, while physical expressions of worship can release bodily tension. Lastly, many believe in the power of divine healing that can occur during worship, encompassing physical, emotional, and spiritual realms.

By focusing on these aspects, you can convey how worship can be a holistic and transformative healing experience. Healing in worship can be a profound experience, encompassing spiritual, emotional, and even physical aspects. Here are some key ways worship can facilitate healing:

Spiritual Renewal

Worship often involves connecting with a higher power, which can provide a sense of spiritual renewal and peace. This connection can help individuals feel supported and cared for, fostering a sense of wholeness and healing.

Emotional Release

Worship provides a safe space for expressing emotions. Singing, praying, and meditating allow individuals to release pent-up emotions, which can be cathartic and healing. This emotional release can help in processing grief, pain, and stress.

Sense of Community

Participating in worship with others creates a sense of community and belonging. This communal support can be incredibly healing, as it provides a network of care and mutual support. Knowing that others are praying for you and supporting you can be comforting and uplifting.

Reflection and Introspection

Worship often includes periods of quiet reflection and introspection. This time allows individuals to contemplate their lives, acknowledge their struggles, and seek guidance. Such introspection can lead to personal insights and emotional healing.

Positive Affirmations

Worship frequently involves affirmations of faith, hope, and love. These positive affirmations can replace negative thoughts and feelings, promoting a healthier and more optimistic outlook on life.

Ritual and Routine

The rituals and routines of worship can provide stability and comfort. Regular participation in worship can create a sense of normalcy and predictability, which is particularly healing during times of chaos or uncertainty.

Physical Expression

Some forms of worship involve physical movement, such as dancing, bowing, or clapping. These physical expressions can help release tension and stress, contributing to overall physical and emotional well-being.

Divine Healing

Many believe in the power of divine intervention during worship. Prayers for healing, oil anointing, and other sacred services are thought to invite divine healing, which can manifest in physical, emotional, or spiritual ways.

Declare and Decree the Scriptures

1. **Jeremiah 17:14**: Heal me, O Lord, and I shall be healed; save me, and I shall be saved, for you are my praise.

2. **Jeremiah 30:17**: But I will restore you to health and heal your wounds,' declares the LORD, 'because you are called an outcast, Zion for whom no one cares.

3. **Jeremiah 33:6**: Behold, I will bring to it health and healing, and I will heal them and reveal to them abundance of prosperity and security.

4. **Psalm 6:2**: Be gracious to me, O Lord, for I am languishing; heal me, O Lord, for my bones are troubled.

5. **Psalm 41:3**: The Lord sustains him on his sickbed; in his illness you restore him to full health.

6. **Psalm 103:2-3**: Bless the Lord, O my soul, and forget not all his benefits, who forgives all your iniquity, who heals all your diseases,

7. **Psalm 147:3**: He heals the brokenhearted and binds up their wounds.

8. **Proverbs 17:22**: A joyful heart is good medicine, but a crushed spirit dries up the bones.

9. **James 5:15**: And the prayer of faith will save the one who is sick, and the Lord will raise him up. And if he has committed sins, he will be forgiven.

10. **1 Peter 2:24**: He himself bore our sins in his body on the tree, that we might die to sin and live to righteousness. By His wounds you have been healed.

11. **3 John 1:2**: Beloved, I pray that all may go well with you and that you may be in good health, as it goes well with your soul.

Prayer for Healing

Father,

Help me to keep my focus on You when the pain and hurt are overwhelming. Help me be faithful and see the good and blessings surrounding me. Please strengthen my mind, heart, and body, and heal me today. May the Holy Spirit guide me in peace and comfort. Amen.

Notes

DAY 15

Worship That Causes You to Rest

Worship that leads us to rest in God's presence brings deep peace, comfort, and renewal, allowing us to release our burdens and experience the Holy Spirit's sustaining presence. The prayer "Spirit of the Living God, rest on us" reflects a yearning for God's Spirit to dwell intimately with us, bringing rest to our souls and transforming our hearts and minds.

Rest in the Presence
Matthew 11:28-29

Come to me, all you who are weary and burdened, and I will give you rest. Take my yoke upon you and learn from me, for I am gentle and humble in heart, and you will find rest for your souls."

True rest comes when we come to Jesus in worship, laying down our anxieties, stresses, and concerns. As we worship, we surrender to His gentle care and allow His Spirit to lift our burdens, giving us rest and refreshing our souls.

The Spirit of God Brings Rest
Isaiah 63:14

"Like cattle that go down to the plain, they were given rest by the Spirit of the Lord. This is how you guided your people to make for yourself a glorious name."

Interpretation: The Spirit of the Lord is the one who gives rest. When the Holy Spirit rests on us, we experience a deep sense of peace, guidance, and protection, similar to how God led the Israelites with His presence. In worship, we open ourselves to the Holy Spirit's comfort and guidance, allowing Him to still our hearts.

Worship in Stillness and Trust
Psalm 46:10

Be still, and know that I am God; I will be exalted among the nations, I will be exalted in the earth.

Interpretation: Worship that leads to rest often involves stillness and trust in God. In a world filled with noise and distractions, worship provides an opportunity to pause and rest in the knowledge of God's sovereignty and faithfulness. As we rest in Him, we allow the Holy Spirit to work in us, calming our fears and filling us with divine peace.

Rest from Striving
Hebrews 4:9-10

There remains, then, a Sabbath rest for the people of God; for anyone who enters God's rest also rests from their works, just as God did from his.

Worship is a space where we stop striving in our own strength and rest in the finished work of Christ. The "Sabbath rest" represents a deeper spiritual rest, where we trust in God's grace rather than our own efforts. Through worship, we cease from anxious striving and rely on the power of the Holy Spirit to sustain and renew us.

The Spirit as Our Comforter
John 14:26-27

But the Advocate, the Holy Spirit, whom the Father will send in my name, will teach you all things and will remind you of everything I have said to you. Peace, I leave with you; my peace I give you. I do not give to you as the world gives. Do not let your hearts be troubled and do not be afraid."

Interpretation: The Holy Spirit, described as the Advocate or Comforter, brings peace and rest to our souls. In worship, we invite the Spirit to dwell in us, and as He does, we experience the peace of Christ that surpasses all understanding—a peace that the world cannot give.

Rest Through Trusting God's Plan
Jeremiah 29:11

"For I know the plans I have for you," declares the Lord, "plans to prosper you and not to harm you, plans to give you hope and a future."

Worship that causes us to rest often includes surrendering our plans and trusting God's perfect will for our lives. As we worship, we remind ourselves of God's promises and rest in the assurance that He is in control and has a good plan for us.

Letting Go and Resting in Worship
1 Peter 5:7

Cast all your anxiety on Him because He cares for you.

Interpretation: Worship is a time to let go of our worries, doubts, and fears, casting them onto the Lord. When we do this, the Spirit of God fills us with peace, taking the weight of our burdens and enabling us to rest in His love and care.

Spirit-Led Worship Brings Refreshing
Acts 3:19-20

Repent, then, and turn to God, so that your sins may be wiped out, that times of refreshing may come from the Lord, and that He may send the Messiah, who has been appointed for you—even Jesus.

Interpretation: Times of refreshing and renewal come when we turn to God in worship, confessing our need for Him and seeking His presence. The Holy Spirit refreshes and revives us as we worship, bringing new strength, clarity, and peace.

When we invite the Holy Spirit to rest upon us in worship, we open ourselves to divine peace, renewal, and rest that goes beyond mere physical relaxation. Worship allows us to lay down our burdens and rest in God's presence, trusting in His love and care. In that place of surrender, the Spirit of the Living God refreshes our souls, calming our hearts and giving us the strength we need for the journey ahead.

Notes

___
___
___
___
___
___
___
___
___
___
___

DAY 16

The Heart of True Worship

The Heart of Worship is intimacy with God through worship. It emphasizes a desire to draw near to God, expressing a heartfelt pursuit of His presence. This is a time of surrender and devotion; it brings you closer to the Father. Worship is the heartbeat of a Christian's relationship with God. It's not just a set of rituals or songs but a deep expression of our love, reverence, and awe of who God is. In both the Old and New Testaments, worship is central to how we connect with God, and it involves surrendering our hearts, minds and lives to Him.

1. Worship is a Response to God's Greatness
In Psalm 95:6, the psalmist writes, "Come, let us bow down in worship, let us kneel before the Lord our Maker; for He is our God, and we are the people of His pasture, the flock under His care."

True worship begins with recognizing who God is—our Creator, Shepherd, and King. It's a response to His majesty, power, and love. When we worship, we acknowledge His greatness and submit to His authority.

2. Worship is a Lifestyle, Not an Event

Romans 12:1 teaches, "Therefore, I urge you, brothers and sisters, in view of God's mercy, to offer your bodies as a living sacrifice, holy and pleasing to God—this is your true and proper worship."

Worship isn't limited to what happens in church on Sunday. It is something we live out daily by offering ourselves to God. Every decision we make, every action we take, can be an act of worship when done in obedience and surrender to God.

3. Worship in Spirit and in Truth

In John 4:24, Jesus says, "God is spirit, and His worshipers must worship in the Spirit and in truth." True worship is not about the external—it's about the condition of the heart. Worship must be sincere, led by the Holy Spirit, and rooted in the truth of who God is. It's not just about following traditions or going through the motions but about engaging our hearts and minds in genuine reverence for God.

4. Worship Brings Us Closer to God

James 4:8 promises: Come near to God and He will come near to you. When we worship, we draw near to God, and He responds by drawing near to us. Worship opens our hearts to experience God's presence in deeper ways, bringing us comfort, peace, and joy. It aligns our hearts with His will and reminds us of His constant presence in our lives.

5. Worship Transforms Us

In 2 Corinthians 3:18, Paul writes, **"And we all, who with unveiled faces contemplate the Lord's glory, are being transformed into His image with ever-increasing glory."**

As we worship, we are transformed. Focusing on God's glory and goodness changes us from the inside out. Worship reshapes our priorities, renews our minds, and strengthens our faith.

Prayer

Father,

We come before You with humble hearts, desiring to worship You in spirit and truth. Help us to recognize Your greatness and offer ourselves entirely to You. May our lives reflect Your glory, and may our worship draw us closer to You. Transform us as we seek Your face and give You all the honor and praise. In Jesus' name, Amen.

Worship is an opportunity to offer your heart to God each day, knowing that as you do, He will draw near, fill you with His presence, and transform your life.

Write your prayer for worship below:

DAY 17

Learning Other Types of Worship

Worship can take many forms; each providing unique ways to express and experience faith devotion, and spirituality.

- **Liturgical Worship**

- **Non-Liturgical Worship**

- **Contemporary Worship**

- **Charismatic Worship**

- **Traditional Worship**

- **Private Worship**

- **Family Worship**

- **Corporate Worship**

- **Sacramental Worship**

- **Interfaith Worship**

- **Nature Worship**

- **Contemplative Worship**

By exploring these various forms, you can understand how people connect with their faith and express their devotion. Here is a more in-depth look at some of the different types of worship:

1. Liturgical Worship

Liturgical worship follows a set structure and rituals, often outlined in a formal liturgy. This type is common in denominations like Roman Catholicism, Eastern Orthodoxy, and Anglicanism. It includes readings, hymns, prayers, and sacraments (such as the Eucharist).

2. Non-Liturgical Worship

Non-liturgical worship is less structured and allows for more spontaneity. It is common in many Protestant denominations, such as Baptists and Pentecostals. Services may include extemporaneous prayers, spontaneous singing, and impromptu testimonies.

3. Contemporary Worship

Contemporary worship uses modern music, multimedia, and informal settings to create an engaging worship experience. It often takes place in evangelical and non-denominational churches and aims to appeal to a younger audience with contemporary songs and a relaxed atmosphere.

4. Charismatic Worship

Charismatic worship is marked by enthusiastic and expressive forms of worship, including speaking in tongues, prophecy, healing, and lively music. This style is prevalent in Pentecostal and charismatic movements.

5. Traditional Worship

Traditional worship incorporates classic hymns, formal prayers, and established rituals. It often reflects long-standing religious practices and is found in many mainline Protestant denominations.

6. Private/Personal Worship

Personal worship involves individual practices such as prayer, meditation, Bible reading, and personal reflection. This form allows individuals to connect with their faith in a more intimate and personalized way.

7. Family Worship

Family worship is practiced at home, involving family members in collective prayer, scripture reading, and discussion. It helps to build spiritual bonds within the family and nurture faith from a young age.

8. Corporate Worship

Corporate worship refers to communal gatherings for worship, such as Sunday services, where a congregation comes together to worship as a unified body. It emphasizes community and collective expressions of faith.

9. Sacramental Worship

Sacramental worship focuses on the observance of sacred rites, such as baptism and communion. These sacraments are considered outward signs of inward grace and are central to traditions like Catholicism, Orthodoxy, and some Protestant denominations.

10. Interfaith Worship

Interfaith worship involves individuals from different religious traditions coming together to pray, meditate, or celebrate shared values. This type promotes understanding and cooperation among various faith communities.

11. Nature Worship

Nature worship connects with the divine through the natural world. Practices may include meditative walks, outdoor services, and rituals that honor creation. This type of worship is common in indigenous religions and some modern spiritual movements.

12. Contemplative Worship

Contemplative worship focuses on silence, meditation, and contemplative prayer. It aims to foster deep inner stillness and awareness of the divine presence. This form is practiced in monastic traditions and by individuals seeking a quiet, reflective spiritual experience.

Notes

DAY 18

Personal vs. Corporate Worship

Both personal and corporate worship are vital aspects of the Christian life, but they serve different purposes and dynamics. Let's explore the differences and the importance of each:

- **Personal Worship**: Focuses on individual devotion to God, including prayer, reading scripture, and personal acts of praise and adoration.

- **Corporate Worship**: Worship as part of a community or congregation, especially in the church setting. Explore the significance of communal worship as outlined in Hebrews 10:25 and how it strengthens the faith of the body of Christ.

Personal Worship

Personal worship refers to the individual act of connecting with God, where believers seek to praise, honor, and commune with God in their own private time. It includes personal prayer, Bible reading, reflection, meditation, and singing praise to God. Personal worship can take place anywhere–at home, while walking, or even in the workplace.

Key Elements of Personal Worship:

- **Private Relationship with God**: It is deeply personal, often reflecting one's individual relationship with God. Jesus speaks of this in Matthew 6:6, encouraging believers to pray in secret, where the Father sees and rewards.

- **Spontaneity and Flexibility**: Personal worship allows for flexibility. You can worship whenever and wherever you feel led without any constraints of time or form.

- **Deepening Intimacy**: Personal worship fosters intimacy with God. It allows space for quiet reflection, heartfelt prayer, confession, and a personal connection with the Holy Spirit.

- **Self-Examination and Growth**: During personal worship, believers are more likely to engage in self-reflection, seeking to align their lives with God's will, grow spiritually, and gain personal insights into their walk with God.

- **Focus on Personal Needs and Gratitude**: It often revolves around one's personal life, struggles, thanksgiving, and desires to hear God's voice for individual direction.

Scriptural Example of Personal Worship:

- **David**: King David is a strong example of personal worship, seen in many of the Psalms. In Psalm 63:1, David speaks of seeking God in solitude: "O God, You are my God; Early will I seek You; My soul thirsts for You."

- **Jesus**: Jesus often withdrew to quiet places for prayer (Luke 5:16), showing the importance of personal time with the Father.

Benefits of Personal Worship:

- **Spiritual Growth**: Personal worship helps deepen one's understanding of God and the Scriptures, leading to maturity in faith.

- **Peace and Strength**: It provides peace, clarity, and spiritual strength in daily life, especially during difficult times.

- **Constant Fellowship**: Personal worship cultivates a continuous relationship with God, helping believers remain grounded in Him.

Describe Your Encounter with the Father

The following scriptures highlight the essence of personal worship–a deeply intimate and ongoing connection with God through prayer, praise, reflection, and surrender. Personal worship allows us to experience God's presence, hear His voice, and offer our lives as living sacrifices to Him. It is through these individual acts of devotion that our personal relationship with God is deepened and strengthened. Study the following scriptures on personal worship that emphasize the importance of individual devotion, prayer, and relationship with God:

1. Matthew 6:6 (NIV)

But when you pray, go into your room, close the door, and pray to your Father, who is unseen. Then your Father, who sees what is done in secret, will reward you.

Interpretation: Jesus encourages personal, private worship, highlighting the importance of a direct relationship with God, away from public attention or recognition.

2. Psalm 63:1 (NIV) You, God, are my God, earnestly I seek you; I thirst for you, my whole being longs for you, in a dry and parched land where there is no water.

Interpretation: David expresses his deep, personal longing for God in this psalm, showing how personal worship involves earnestly seeking God with all of our hearts.

3. Psalm 42:1-2 (NIV) "As the deer pants for streams of water, so my soul pants for you, my God. My soul thirsts for God, for the living God. When can I go and meet with God?

Interpretation: This passage portrays a deep, personal desire for God, symbolizing personal worship as a longing for God's presence.

4. Romans 12:1 (NIV) Therefore, I urge you, brothers and sisters, in view of God's mercy, to offer your bodies as a living sacrifice, holy and pleasing to God–this is your true and proper worship.

Interpretation: Worship is not confined to a specific time or place. Personal worship involves offering your entire life to God as an act of devotion and surrender.

5. Psalm 16:11 (NIV) You make known to me the path of life; you will fill me with joy in your presence, with eternal pleasures at your right hand.

Interpretation: This scripture emphasizes the joy and fulfillment that come from spending personal time in God's presence.

6. Psalm 119:105 (NIV) Your word is a lamp for my feet, a light on my path.

Interpretation: In personal worship, we seek God through His Word. Scripture guides our lives, providing wisdom and direction for our personal walk with Him.

7. Mark 1:35 (NIV) Very early in the morning, while it was still dark, Jesus got up, left the house, and went off to a solitary place, where he prayed.

Interpretation: Jesus regularly sought personal time with the Father in prayer, providing an example of the importance of personal worship in solitude.

8. Psalm 27:4 (NIV) One thing I ask from the Lord, this only do I seek: that I may dwell in the house of the Lord all the days of my life, to gaze on the beauty of the Lord and to seek him in his temple.

Interpretation: David's desire for personal worship is seen in his longing to seek God continually, to be in His presence, and to meditate on His beauty.

9. Philippians 4:6-7 (NIV) Do not be anxious about anything, but in every situation, by prayer and petition, with thanksgiving, present your requests to God. And the peace of God, which transcends all understanding, will guard your hearts and your minds in Christ Jesus.

Interpretation: Personal worship through prayer brings peace and strengthens our relationship with God, as we lay our burdens and anxieties before Him.

10. Psalm 34:1 (NIV) I will extol the Lord at all times; his praise will always be on my lips.

Interpretation: Personal worship is a constant attitude of praise and devotion to God, not just confined to specific moments but a continual offering of thanks and worship.

11. James 4:8 (NIV) "Come near to God and he will come near to you. Wash your hands, you sinners, and purify your hearts, you double-minded.

Interpretation: This verse emphasizes the importance of drawing close to God in personal worship. When we intentionally seek Him, He promises to draw near to us.

12. Psalm 91:1-2 (NIV) Whoever dwells in the shelter of the Most High will rest in the shadow of the Almighty. I will say of the Lord, 'He is my refuge and my fortress, my God, in whom I trust.

Interpretation: Personal worship involves dwelling in God's presence and finding rest, security, and trust in Him as our protector and guide.

Notes

_____
_____
_____
_____
_____
_____
_____
_____
_____
_____

DAY 19

Corporate Worship

Corporate worship is the gathering of believers to worship God together as a community, usually in a church setting. It involves collective prayer, singing, reading of Scripture, preaching, and participating in sacraments such as communion. The community aspect of corporate worship is central to the life of the church.

Key Elements of Corporate Worship:

- **Community and Fellowship**: Corporate worship brings believers together as a family, fostering unity and shared faith. It reflects the biblical teaching that the body of Christ is meant to gather and worship together (Hebrews 10:25).

- **Unity in Worship**: When believers come together in worship, there is a unique sense of unity. Jesus promised that where two or three gather in His name, He is there in their midst (Matthew 18:20).

- **Teaching and Exhortation**: Corporate worship includes preaching and teaching, which helps the congregation grow in understanding and faith. The community learns together through the exposition of God's Word.

- **Corporate Prayer and Intercession**: Worship as a body allows for collective intercession and prayer for the needs of the church, community, and the world.

- **Sacraments and Ordinances**: Corporate worship is where believers participate in important practices such as communion (Lord's Supper) and baptism, which are central to the faith.

Scriptural Example of Corporate Worship:

- **Early Church**: Acts 2:42-47 describes the early Christian church gathering regularly for teaching, fellowship, breaking of bread, and prayers. The corporate aspect of worship was foundational to their community life.

- **Israel's Festivals**: The Old Testament is filled with examples of Israel gathering together for corporate worship during festivals and special events (e.g., the Feast of Tabernacles, Passover), reflecting the communal nature of worship.

Benefits of Corporate Worship:

- **Spiritual Strength and Encouragement**: Corporate worship provides encouragement, accountability, and mutual edification. When believers worship together, they strengthen one another's faith.

- **Experiencing God's Presence Collectively**: There is often a unique manifestation of God's presence in the corporate gathering that believers may not experience alone. The collective worship of the church can create a powerful atmosphere for encountering God.

- **Public Witness**: Corporate worship is a testimony to the world. It publicly declares the unity and devotion of the Christian community to God.

- **Participation in the Body of Christ**: Corporate worship allows individuals to experience the broader body of Christ. Worshiping together reminds us that we are part of a larger community of believers with a shared mission and faith.

Comparison and Interconnection

Aspect	Personal Worship	Corporate Worship
Focus	Individual relationship with God	Collective worship and unity in the body of Christ
Setting	Anywhere, any time	Church or group setting
Expression	Spontaneous, personal, and reflective	Structured and often led by a worship leader
Role of Scripture	Personal Bible study and reflection	Collective teaching and preaching of the Word
Spiritual Growth	Focus on personal growth, self-examination	Growth through fellowship, accountability, and mutual edification
Purpose	Deepening personal intimacy with God	Strengthening the community, public testimony, and shared worship
Sacraments	Usually absent in personal worship	Includes baptism and communion
Prayers	Personal prayers and thanksgiving	Corporate prayer and intercession for broader needs

How Personal and Corporate Worship Complement Each Other:

1. **Balanced Worship Life**: Both forms of worship are necessary. Personal worship nurtures a deep, intimate connection with God, while corporate worship allows for fellowship, accountability, and collective edification.

2. **Spiritual Rhythm**: Personal worship throughout the week prepares the heart for corporate worship on Sundays or during church services. Regular corporate worship, in turn, energizes and inspires personal devotion during the week.

3. **Strength in Unity**: Personal worship helps believers develop personal maturity, while corporate worship reminds them that they are part of a larger body–the church. The strength of individual worshipers contributes to the strength of the corporate worship experience.

Both personal and corporate worship play essential roles in the Christian life. Personal worship nurtures an individual's relationship with God, promoting spiritual growth, intimacy, and reliance on the Holy Spirit. Corporate worship, on the other hand, unites the body of believers in praise, teaching, and mutual encouragement, fostering a sense of community and shared mission. Together, these forms of worship provide a balanced and holistic approach to honoring and glorifying God in every aspect of life.

DAY 20

A Worship Leader Carries a Unique Sound

A worship leader carries a unique sound, which goes beyond music—it's a spiritual expression that conveys the heart and presence of God in a way that touches the congregation. This "sound" is a combination of their personal relationship with God, their spiritual sensitivity, and the unique calling of the house or church they serve in. Here's how this concept breaks down:

1. **Spiritual Authority**: The worship leader carries authority in the atmosphere. Their sound has the ability to shift atmospheres and bring people into a place of worship, intimacy, and surrender to God.

2. **Alignment with God's Spirit**: Worship leaders must be in tune with what God is doing in the moment. This means listening to His Spirit and allowing their sound to reflect His will for the congregation in real-time.

3. **Unique to the House**: Each house or church has a specific sound—a spiritual identity. The worship leader's sound must align with that identity, helping to amplify the unique expression of worship in that community.

4. **Heart and Intention**: The sound they carry isn't just musical excellence; it's rooted in their personal walk with God, their humility, and their desire to lead others into God's presence.

5. **Flow of the Spirit**: A worship leader's sound must flow with the Spirit, creating a space where the congregation can encounter God in a deep and meaningful way.

A worship leader who carries the right sound brings the church into alignment with what God is speaking to that community. They are responsible for nurturing the sound that breaks chains, brings healing, and leads people into God's presence. This prayer is a way to invite God to lead and guide the sound of worship, ensuring it carries His presence and impacts the lives of all who hear it.

A Prayer for the Sound in Worship:

Heavenly Father,

We thank You for the gift of worship and for those You've appointed to lead Your people into Your presence. Today, we lift up the sound that comes from Your house, a sound that carries Your heart, Your spirit, and Your power. Lord, we ask that You anoint every worship leader, musician, and vocalist with a fresh outpouring of Your Holy Spirit. Let their hearts be completely surrendered to

You, so the sound they carry is not their own but a reflection of Your glory and Your will.

Align Their Sound With Heaven:

Father, let the sound they release reflect the sound of Heaven. Let it be filled with purity, peace, and power. Tune their hearts to hear Your voice and guide them to release the exact sound needed for this time and season.

Breakthrough and Healing:

Lord, let their sound be a weapon of warfare in the spiritual realm. As they worship, let strongholds be broken, chains be loosed, and healing flow. Release Your power through the sound to restore hearts, heal bodies, and deliver minds.

Unity and Alignment:

Father, let the sound in the house be one of unity. Let the worship team move in one spirit and one accord, so the sound they create brings the congregation into perfect alignment with Your will. Let there be no division but a unified sound that resonates with Your heart for this house.

Protection and Purity:

We pray for protection over the worship team, that the enemy would have no foothold in their lives. Guard their hearts, keep them humble, and protect their purity, so the sound they carry remains undefiled and holy unto You.

Release Creativity and Fresh Anointing:

God, we ask for a fresh release of creativity and anointing. Birth new songs, new sounds, and new expressions of worship that reflect what You are doing in this season. Give them the boldness to step into the new things You are calling them to carry.

Father, we thank You for the sound that comes from Your house. May it always glorify You, lead Your people into deeper intimacy, and carry Your power to transform lives. In Jesus' mighty name, we pray. Amen

Notes

_____
_____
_____
_____
_____
_____
_____
_____
_____
_____
_____
_____
_____
_____

DAY 21

I Am Who God Says I Am

The following affirmations for worship leaders are designed to encourage, uplift, and remind them of their calling and purpose in leading worship. These affirmations help keep the hearts of worship leaders grounded in their purpose and remind them that their ministry is a reflection of God's presence and power.

1. I am anointed by God to lead His people into His presence.

2. The Holy Spirit guides me in every song, every note, and every moment of worship.

3. I carry the sound of heaven in my worship.

4. I am sensitive to the voice of God, and I follow His leading in worship.

5. I am equipped to shift atmospheres through the sound I release.

6. My worship creates a space for God's presence to move powerfully.

7. I am called to lead others into deeper intimacy with God.

8. Every song I sing is an offering of praise to the King of Kings.

9. I carry a unique sound that is meant to bless the body of Christ.

10. God's love and grace flow through me as I lead worship.

11. I am humble before God, knowing He is the true focus of worship.

12. I walk in purity and integrity, reflecting Christ in my worship.

13. God uses my voice and my gifts to break chains and bring freedom.

14. I am a vessel for God's presence, and His Spirit works through me.

15. The songs I release carry healing, peace, and restoration.

16. I am a conduit of God's heart for His people, through every note and melody.

17. My worship is a weapon of spiritual warfare, and God fights through my praise.

18. I am an instrument of God's glory, and I magnify His name in every gathering.

19. The joy of the Lord is my strength as I lead others in praise and worship.

20. I continually grow in my craft and calling as a worship leader.

21. God's presence goes before me, and His glory surrounds every moment of worship.

MEET THE AUTHOR

Helen Marie Jones

Helen M. Jones is a Pastor, Prophet, Psalmist, Encourager, Intercessor, Mentor, and an Anointed Worship Leader/Levite who leads people into the Presence of God. She aspires to inspire others to worship God and to make a positive impact in the lives of His people. Apostle Helen is the Senior Pastor & Founder, along with her husband, Bishop Arbin Jones, of Divine Worship Center, located in Gray Court, SC. She is the mother of three daughters: Shemika, Jasmine, and Marjorie, and she has ten beautiful grandchildren. Apostle Helen is the founder and visionary of **Sister 2 Sister Ministries**, where she builds and empowers women, families, and teens who are broken and abused, helping them find their way to live again. In 2023, Apostle Helen became a Certified Life Coach to help young men and women **S.H.I.F.T.** into their fullest potential in life. She is a woman of faith and is sure to shift any atmosphere she encounters. She is also the founder of the Facebook Live 5 a.m. **"Morning**

Awakening," a power hour of prayer, praise, and worship. Additionally, Pastor Helen is the founder of **HMJ Ministries**, whose motto is: *United in Prayer, United in Strength, Victorious in Battle.* Apostle Helen maintains an atmosphere of transparency, integrity, authenticity, and excellence, which has enabled her to serve effectively. She lives by John 4:24: *"God is a Spirit, and they that worship Him must worship Him in spirit and in truth."* She believes that through the Word of God and worship, deliverance will take place, and souls will be saved and set free.

Made in the USA
Columbia, SC
02 June 2025